A
Countryside
of
Verse

ISBN: 1 872547 41 9

Poems: Copyright Richard W. Farrall © 1994

Illustrations: Copyright Angela Scott © 1994

Published by Sherbourne Publications
Sweeney Mountain, Oswestry,
Shropshire SY10 9EX, UK

Set in New Century Schoolbook

Typesetting and Printing by
Clarkeprint Ltd., Waveney House,
45-47 Stour Street, Ladywood, Birmingham B18 7AJ

Also in Softback ISBN: 1 872547 46 X

A Countryside of Verse

by

Richard W. Farrall

Illustrated by Angela Scott

Sherbourne Publications

To Carol

THE OAK TREE

I stood beneath a broadleaved oak,
And rested in its shadowy cloak,
Its branches spread above my head,
And higher still the sun burnt red.
While in the cool its shade had brought,
Into my mind there came a thought,
How very small and frail seemed I
Beside this giant that touched the sky.
How very short my life would be
Compared to this old, graceful tree.
How many seasons had it seen,
Of Autumn falls and Summers green.
What tales to tell if it could speak,
Of Spring-time lambs and Winters bleak.
Of men that rose before the dawn,
And then with horses cut the corn.
But now the horse and ox are gone,
It's progress now that marches on.
And oh what changes there have been,
And oh what memories could you glean.
But all these years that mighty tree
Has not a single thought set free.
But still it looks with unseen eye,
As man and time go passing by.

BOB

He gazes out across the fields,
His vision dull and blurred,
And cocks an ear expectantly
For whistle or for word.

But Bob hears none, for he is old,
And long, long, been retired,
It's many a day since Bob's help
Has been for work required.

The words "Come-by, away, lie down,"
No longer fill his day,
For now there is but one command,
And that command is "Stay."

It's Jim who works the sheep these days,
He's young, and fit, and keen,
He's eager and he's very brave,
Just as old Bob had been.

But when the day is at its close,
And with it comes the night,
The Farmer beckons Bob inside
Where all is warm and bright.

To lie upon the old hearth rug
And drift along in sleep,
And dream his dreams of bygone days,
A'working with the sheep.

APRIL

Gently falling April showers,
Washing faces Springtime flowers.
Blackthorn blossom softly falling,
Up above the pigeons calling.
In the hedge-rows chaffinch sing,
Swallows low upon the wing.
Busy buzzing bumble bees,
Amid the flowering cherry trees.
Primrose growing yellow cluster,
Pheasant cocks, all bluff and bluster.
Spiky gorses golden finger,
On the meadow, curlews linger.
Missel-thrush upon the nest,
As soon will be the golden-crest.
Blackbirds courting on the lawn,
Magpies nest in thickest thorn.
Fluffy gosling hatching out,
Goose and gander screech and shout.
Snow white lambs that run and play,
This and more – an April day.

THE HOSTLER

When I was younger than today,
I met a man called Albert Gray.
How old he was I could not say,
But many years had passed his way.
With painful gait he slowly walked,
In gentle whispers, softly talked.
Who told me tales of yester-year,
Painted images bright and clear,
Of teams of Shires, in shaft and chain,
That worked the land through sun and rain.
The Suffolk Punch and clanking plough,
An ancient art forgotten now.
Of Cleveland Bays, a matching pair,
The colourful Gypsy at Appleby Fair.
A majestic stallion, black as coal,
A chestnut mare and filly foal.
Of yearling colts that he had known,
And gentle giants he'd called his own.
He'd loved them all, but all had gone,
The Clydesdale and the Percheron.
But still the fire burned in his eyes,
A love that lasts and never dies.

SWALLOW'S RETURN

Welcome back my little friend,
On you I knew I could depend.
How many miles have you flown,
To reach your English Summer home.
What sights to see along the way,
To greet me now this April day.
Above the plains of foreign lands,
And over burning Sahara sands.
Through storm and tempest, wind and rain,
Your wings have brought you home again.

THE VIXEN AND THE EWE

Morning breaks with the sun, it is an April dawn,
And down upon the meadow, a new life has been born.
A snow white lamb, greets the world with a wanton bleat,
And with his first uncertain steps, scrambles to his feet.
The kindly ewe, with gentle eye, looks down with honest pride,
Upon her new born lamb, a-nuzzling by her side.
Instinctively, for Mother's milk, he searches for her udder,
With wag of tail, triumphantly, he suckles from his mother.

In a woodland far away, sun filters through the trees,
Down into the brambles, the bracken, and the leaves.
Dug deep into a sandy bank, there is a foxes earth,
And far within its vaults, a vixen's given birth.
Her four blind whelps, helpless, she tends their every need,
Whilst they upon her milk, do satisfy their greed.
She alone will raise the litter, all throughout the Summer,
With all her loving care, and devotion of a Mother.

Spring draws to a close, it is the month of May,
The lamb upon the meadow, happy in his play.
But hidden in a hedge-row, the vixen watches on,
Four hungry cubs must be fed, before the day is done.
The watchful ewe sees the vixen make her dash,
Rushes to her lamb, stamping foot upon the grass.
The vixen knows all is lost, returning to her cover.
The ewe has won this day, but there will be another.

MAY

Walk in woodland early morning,
Hear a distant cuckoo calling.
Waves and waves of blue bell heads,
Trees in blossom, pink and reds.
Squirrels scamper high above,
Softly cooing collared dove.
Chiffchaff sings in silver birches,
Noisy rooks on lofty perches.
Speckled wooded butterflies,
Flit through branches to the skies.
Sitting broody pheasant hens.
Willow-warblers, little wrens.
Nuthatch nests in ancient ash,
Rabbits peer, then quickly dash.
And little fox cubs out to play,
Revel in the sun of May.

FARMERS' FOLLY

Michael on his tractor rides,
Sprays the land with pesticides,
Another primrose slowly dies.
He knows not what he's done.

Simon fells another tree,
To further productivity,
The robin's nest he does not see,
Nor does he even care.

Judy dreams of catalogue pages,
Feeds the hens in battery cages,
Mini skirts are all the rage as
She ignores the pain.

Bureaucrats in office towers,
Nine to five their office hours,
Rubber plants and plastic flowers,
Farm policy decree.

Politicians go to lobby,
Ivor's loaded up his lorry,
Full of lambs, so sad and sorry,
For slaughter far away.

They never stop to reason why,
To market forces they'll comply,
But there will come a time to cry,
For all that they have done.

THE FOAL

Tell me, tell me, little man,
Answer me, if you can,
What thoughts are with you as you play,
Upon this warm and sunny day.
You think yourself so very brave,
A naughty foal, who won't behave.
And do concern your Mother so,
As you gallop too and fro.
But run and play, whilst you can,
And sleep a while, little man.
Too soon these carefree days will pass,
Of Mother's milk, and Summer's grass.

NESTING

Architects with mud and straw,
Lapwings nesting on the floor.
Graceful swallows through the air,
Lining their nests with horses' hair.
Idle crows with twigs make do,
To lay their eggs of greenish-blue.
Upon her throne, a regal swan,
Counts her eggs, one by one.
From afar, there comes a'tapping,
Upon a tree, a beak is rapping.
Mallard in amongst the rushes,
On a bough, the missel-thrushes.
Swifts are high, beneath the eaves,
Tiny goldcrests in the leaves.
All are building, all are nesting,
Only one bird now is resting.
In a tree that stands so tall,
Now is heard the cuckoo's call.

THE SALMON

Below the rushing weir's cascade,
Where the billowing foam is made.
And the river's heard to roar,
This is where the salmon soar.
Time and time again they leap,
Against the water that is steep.
Amid its spray and mossy rocks,
Were willows train their leafy locks.
Then run the gauntlet of the stand,
Where poachers wait, with gaff in hand.
And fishermen who chance their luck,
With garish hackle and barbed hook.
Past an island made of silt,
That over years, time has built.
Through the shallows, they will swim,
Plume the water with dorsal fin.
On and on, they forge ahead,
To reach an ancient gravel bed.
Where they themselves, five years before,
Had hatched upon that stoney floor.
A pentad of years they wandered free,
Down the river, and far to sea.
To feed amid the ocean depths,
Before returning, retracing steps.
And face the gruelling river's climb,
As salmon have since dawn of time.

THE FARMYARD CAT

Consider now the farmyard cat.
He sits around just getting fat.
It seems to me a marvellous life,
Without a care, and free of strife.
He wanders free both night and day,
No stable door can bar his way.
He spends his days a sleepy-head,
Upon the hay he makes his bed.
By night he prowls the granary floor,
To hunt the mouse with sharpened claw.
And then perhaps a'courting goes,
To where he travels, no one knows.
Returning home by morning light,
To end another busy night.

THE SKY-LARK

Hear a sky-lark as it flies,
High above, in cloudless skies.
Sweet the smell of new mown hay,
Upon an endless Summer's day.
Catch the scented wild rose,
Upon the breeze, its perfume flows.
See the foxgloves' purple heads,
Scarlet poppies, crimson beds.
Where Painted Lady butterflies,
And Tiger Moths with diamond eyes,
Will flit amid the Summer's bloom,
While hornets hum a constant tune.
Fields of clover, red and white,
Honey bees in laboured flight,
Bearing burdens to the hive,
While graceful swallows swoop and dive.
And all the time the sky-lark sings,
High above on fluttering wings.

MEMORIES

When I was young, and but a boy,
I filled my days with endless joy.
Beside a tranquil pond would sit,
And reel upon my rod would fit.
Then cast a line upon it there,
My eyes upon my float would stare.
Then wait, and hope, and sometimes dream,
Of carp, and tench, and giant bream.
But that was thirty years ago,
Where have they gone, I do not know.

SUMMER TRANCE

Gaze upon a crystal lake,
With time to pause, and time to take.
Beside the flowing willow trees,
That softly sway in Summer breeze.
Watch the Kingfisher as it dives,
And feeds upon the roach that rise.
Hear the noisy moorhen's clicks,
To summon forth her tiny chicks.
In waters cool the carp abound,
While up above the heron's found.
Who stalks the frog amid the reed,
And crested newts in tangled weed.
And as you ponder standing there,
As if by magic through the air,
A brilliant pair of dragonflies,
Weave their magic before your eyes.
Bejewelled, dazzling they will dance,
And cast a spell of summer trance.

15

THE MILL

The ruined mill is standing still,
The wheel no longer turns.
Upon its walls the ivy grows,
Below, the tangled ferns.

Beside its crumbling brickwork flows,
The busy laughing stream.
Reminding us – of what once was,
Like a half-forgotten dream.

Through slateless rotting rafters,
The sunlight down does pour,
Deep amid the eerie gloom,
And onto a sandstone floor.

Where once its beating heart now lies,
The hub of all its power,
The massive granite grinding stone,
Which crushed the wheat to flour.

Whilst cradled in the laughing stream,
Upon a stoney bed,
The giant water-wheel has lain,
To rest its weary head.

No longer does the wheel turn,
No more the stone shall groan,
Abandoned now amongst the ferns,
The old mill stands alone.

THE SCAPEGOAT

Around my neck I'm forced to wear,
A collar secure, does that seem fair?
Tethered out with rope and stake,
In my opinion there's been a mistake.
For I'm obedient, sweet and kind,
A better goat you could not find.

Oh yes, there have been a few mishaps,
But we all suffer the occasional lapse.
And they were not entirely my fault,
After all, a five bar gate is easy to vault.
And while looking for a tasty weed,
How was I to know the cows would stampede!

I truly meant the gander no harm,
But my presence seemed to cause some alarm.
He ran straight onto my horns, that stupid bird,
To say it was intentional, is quite absurd.
About the meal-house, I was wrongly accused,
Open doors are invites, never refused.

It's silly to wrap meal in bags of paper,
A stronger material would be much safer.
One such bag touched the tip of my horn,
And before my eyes did appear all this corn.
Like a waterfall the grain did spill,
And you cannot blame me for eating my fill.

They shouted, swore, chased me out of the granary,
Oh, by the way, what exactly's a cannery?
So now I'm tethered as you can see,
The reason why is a mystery to me.
Putting these minor mishaps aside,
There are some points you just cannot hide.

For I am such a pretty goat,
With flowing beard and silky coat,
Are not my horns the best around?
Is not my bleat the sweetest sound?
So why, Oh why, is this my lot,
To be tethered here in this lonely spot?

THE SPARROW

Little sparrow, if it could be,
That I were you, and you were me.
I'd greet the new day's early dawn,
And feed upon the ripened corn.
Then see the sun rise in the east,
To bid good-day to man and beast.
Then watch mankind go hurrying by,
While I would fly in crowdless sky.
Then see the sun set in the west,
To tell me now it's time to rest.
What think you sparrow, if it could be,
That I were you, and you were me.

THE GALE

Like a sleeping giant waking,
So a mighty storm is breaking.
From afar a mournful wail,
Heralds now the coming gale.
Clouds across the sky will fly,
Like sailing ships they hurry by.
Soon the bullrush bends its head,
The willows on the withe bed.
Like waves upon a stormy shore,
The wheat is battered to the floor.
But the ash tree stands defiant,
And will not bow before the giant.
As if in pain, its branches groan,
Crows nests, from its heights are thrown.
Yet still the ash tree will not cower,
Or yield before the awesome power.
Through the orchard it will roar,
And cast the fruit upon the floor.
It does not care, it shall not spare,
The apple tree, the plum or pear.
And the ash that would not yield,
Now lies smashed upon the field.

A FARMER'S PRAYER

Rain! Rain! Let it rain!
Make the fields green again,
Seed is waiting in the ground,
Hard and baked, no moisture found.
Streams are dry, rocky, bare,
No creature now can water there.
The shady pond, whose waters cool,
Have dwindled down to muddy pool.
Panting sheep all seek the shade,
That mighty oaks and ash have made.
Where are the clouds to fill the sky,
And veil this sun that burns so high?
The land is parched, it seems in pain.
God in heaven, let it rain.

THE MOLE

Busy mole digging down,

Making tunnels in the ground.

He hides away from you and me,

It's said he's blind, and cannot see.

He toils for hours, night and day,

Through lawn and field he makes his way.

No rain can soak his velvet fur,

He does not see the seasons stir.

No frost can chill his tiny feet,

Nor sun upon his back will beat.

The owl and stoat he does not fear,

The cunning fox is never near.

It's true to say he can't be seen,

But all can see where he has been!

AUGUST

Glorious August, halcyon days,
Distant shimmering summer haze.
Harvest mice on ears of grain,
Sleepy winding country lane.
Kestrels hovering in the sky,
The Clouded Yellow butterfly.
Thistle down upon the breeze,
Ripened fruit on orchard trees.
Heavy laden, summer fare,
Apple, damson, plum and pear.
Contented cows who chew the cud,
Playful rabbits skirt the wood.
Meadows where the mushrooms grow,
Evenings when the red skies glow.
Long-eared bats at fading light,
Tawny owls in midnight flight.
When Winter comes I shall remember,
Glorious August, in her splendour.

THANKSGIVING

Oh, sound the bell, for harvest's home,
Come gather thee who hears its tone.
For near a year in fields we toil,
Sow the seed, and till the soil.
Cut the hay, and reap the corn,
Tend the calf, that's newly born.
Shear the sheep, and wrap the wool,
Stack the hay, till barns are full.
Sack the golden grain that pours,
Heavy's the weight on granary floors.
Pick the ripened fruit from trees,
Churn the butter, make the cheese.
All this we do with toil, and sweat,
But now we pause – least we forget.
The one who sends the gentle rain,
The sun to swell the ears of grain.
The one who tends the lamb that's born,
While we're asleep, before the dawn.
So unto an ancient church we'll come,
To mutter thanks for all he's done.
For without his gracious unseen hand,
We could not farm this pleasant land.

JIMMY DONE

Today we buried Jimmy Done,
They'll soon erect a marble stone.
And write upon for all to see,
That Jimmy Done died, ninety three.
But chiselled words are very well,
But cannot a life-story tell.
Of moonless nights, and early dawns,
Rabbit warrens beneath the thorns.
Golden ferrets with pinkish eyes,
Meadows where the partridge flies.
Neglected leafy hazel copse,
Where the cackling pheasant drops.
Hidden pockets, and poachers' guns,
Hedge-rows where the rabbit runs.
Marshes where the mallard feed,
And the snipe hide in the reed.
Giant salmon and baited hooks,
Tickled trout, in laughing brooks.
Private woods with trespass signs,
Magistrates and ten bob fines.
Constables with reddened faces,
Hollow trees, and hidden places.
This was the world of Jimmy Done,
A life they will not carve in stone.
But Winter nights, we'll speak his name,
For n'er we'll see his like again.

NOUGHT'S FOR FREE

In amongst the corn sacks, little feet do scurry,
Here you'll find the field mice, always in a hurry.
Busy, busy, always busy, darting here and there,
To feed upon the barley, the finest country fare.
Dead of night is always best to feed upon the corn,
Many ears of grain to eat before the rays of dawn.
It's harvest home, food for all, and feasting time for mice,
But nought's for free, it never is, and some will pay the price.

As if in dreamland far away, the phantom will appear,
The rabbit to his burrow, his body full of fear.
On silent wing, the grim white reaper, a predator of night,
His ghostly form, it probes the gloom, for somewhere to alight.
Silhouetted in a clear night sky, the old barn looms ahead,
And onto rafters, way up high, his taloned feet do tread.
While down below, amongst the grain, still feast the busy mice,
With hypnotic gaze, he watches them, eyes as cold as ice.

Bellies full, and satisfied, the mice are homeward bound,
To the safety of their nests, deep below the ground.
But still aloft, the barn owl waits, the tension in him mounts,
For time is short, just one chance, the raid is all that counts.
With swift descent, and talons bared, he plummets to the floor,
And in that instant, lost forever, those happy days of yore.
For one small mouse, it is the end, within a deadly grip.
Nought's for free, and he has paid, for the harvest trip.

AUTUMN

Autumn dawns, cool and crisp.
Shrouded morning, swirling mist.
Trees have turned a golden brown,
Leaves are falling softly down.
Brittle twigs the spider treads,
Slowly weaves his silken threads.
'Neath the oak, amid the leaves,
On acorns ripe the Badger feeds.
Squirrels scamper in the hazel,
Finding nuts for Winter's table.
Hedgehogs gather leaves and moss,
Shielding them from bitter frost.
Magpies, jays and missel-thrushes,
Feast on sloes in blackthorn bushes.
Summer's gone and Autumn's here,
With Winter creeping ever near.

FLOWN AWAY

As you walked this Autumn day,
Upon the fields with skies of grey.
Did you hear a warbler sing,
Or see a swift upon the wing?
Were there cooing turtle-doves,
Was a wagtail high above?
Have you heard a cuckoo's call,
Did a swallow rise and fall?
No my friend, not today,
All have left, and flown away.

LONI

With sun a'setting in the west,
Now I lay my friend to rest.
Upon the field where sheep still graze,
Where often she did sit and gaze.
Beside the pond where she had swum,
Along whose banks she'd often run.
No longer by my side she'll walk,
Or raise an ear as I talk.
Never again she'll gather sheep,
Nor lie by winter's fire asleep.
Never again a paw she'll raise,
Or I into those eyes will gaze.
The rabbits which she'd always chased,
The hare that she had often raced.
All turn their heads as if to look,
Perhaps they know who heaven's took.

SOWING

A chill wind blows, October beckons,
An angry sky, Winter threatens.
Summer's over, Autumn now,
Time to polish up the plough.
Gone the fields of swaying wheat,
That ripened in the Summer heat.
With harvest safely gathered in,
Now the sowing must begin.
Sea-gulls flock in noisy crowd,
Upon the field that's freshly ploughed.
The seed is waiting to be sown,
Into a rich and fertile loam.
Mother earth awaits her wards,
To keep them safe from Winter's swords.
Protecting all from frosty knives,
Nurturing them till Spring arrives.

WINTER'S SIREN

Winter came a'calling,
One dark December night.
Kissed the land with frosty lips,
Before the morning light.

She painted twisted pictures,
On every window-pane,
Her greeting card she left us,
So all would know her name.

The high-ways and the by-ways,
She polished up like glass,
And cast a million diamonds,
That sparkled in the grass.

The icicle she sculptured,
On every roof and eave.
Upon the unprotected,
Her chilly breath did breathe.

And those of us who in our beds,
Had slept without a care,
Would waken in the morning,
To see that she was there.

HOAR-FROST

A hoar-frost painted filigree,

On every branch, in every tree.

Hedge-rows too, traced in white,

Glisten in the morning light.

Nature works her artistry,

Then unveils for all to see.

But all too soon, to our dismay,

The hoar-frost quickly melts away.

And all that's left are memories,

Of hoar-frost sparkling in the trees.

FEBRUARY

February's upon her throne,
Her reign as cold as any stone.
Now the famine has begun,
All the fruit and berries gone.
Blackthorn stands, stripped and bare,
Gone it's bounteous autumn fare.
Birds will search for dwindling seeds,
Down amongst the crispy leaves.
The pheasant hunched beneath the fronds,
And moor-hens walk on frozen ponds.
Across the fields, bleak and bare,
Denied her cover, the solitary hare.
Flocks of starlings, noisy masses,
Scavenge amidst the frosty grasses.
While hooded crows, with mournful cries,
Watch the sheep with hungry eyes.

THE FOX

A Huntsman's horn, a distant sound,

Horses' hooves on frosty ground.

In the wood, a fox appears,

With baying hounds ever near.

When he was young, he was fast,

But years have come, and quickly past.

His only hope's beneath the ground,

He knows an earth must be found.

A fruitless search, all in vain,

And now the hounds begin to gain.

Nowhere to hide, too tired to run,

The old fox knows his time is come.

If he could speak, I'm sure he'd say,

"It's time whose caught me now this day."

He'll see the hounds, hear their cries,

Snarl at them, then close his eyes.

WINTER'S HAND

Moon is full, stars are bright,
Air is chilled, a Winter's night.
Snow lies soft upon the ground.
There is no wind, there is no sound.
Moonlight falls upon the oak
Her limbs are bare, no emerald cloak.
And all around, a desolate land,
A country gripped by Winter's hand.

In distant wood a vixen screams,
While you and I are lost in dreams.
A sheet of ice, a frozen lake,
The heron cannot hunger slake.
The cunning stoat in winter white,
Will hunt the rabbit through the night.
And in amongst the spruce and larch,
There sits a hare who waits for March.

Beneath the ground and snow so deep,
The dormouse sleeps his winter sleep.
And horseshoe bats in rafters high,
Will hibernate as time goes by.
But both will waken with the Spring,
When Cuckoos call and Warblers sing.
But now they sleep, just like the land,
A country gripped by Winter's hand.

ALMOST SPRING

Spring is near, almost here,
Winter's dying, shed no tear.
Say good-bye to frosty morns,
Welcome now the sunny dawns.
Cast aside dark Winter's night,
Grateful for the evening light.
Forget the bleakest winter scene,
See the fields in velvet green.
Hedges that were brittle stood,
Now the hawthorn starts to bud.
Gone the chilly Winter showers,
Watch the primrose as it flowers.
Ponds that once seemed frozen rock,
Soon abound with tadpole stock.
And empty fields in Winter's waste,
Are filled with lambs that run and chase.

LORD LOOK DOWN

Lord look down upon this place,

And those you call the human race.

You will see what they have done,

Disfigured all that you'd begun.

Would the land cry out in pain?

Poisoned by the acid rain.

Shall you smell the pesticides,

Mourn the fish that slowly dies?

Will you count the whales at sea,

The elephants that once roamed free?

Shall you hear the chain-saws' roar,

That bring the forests to the floor?

Will you marvel at concrete towers,

That man has built upon the flowers?

Lord look down upon this place,

What we have done, is our disgrace.